CREATING COMICS

CREATING FANTASY COMICS

SEB CAMAGAJEVAC

PowerKiDS
press™

NEW YORK

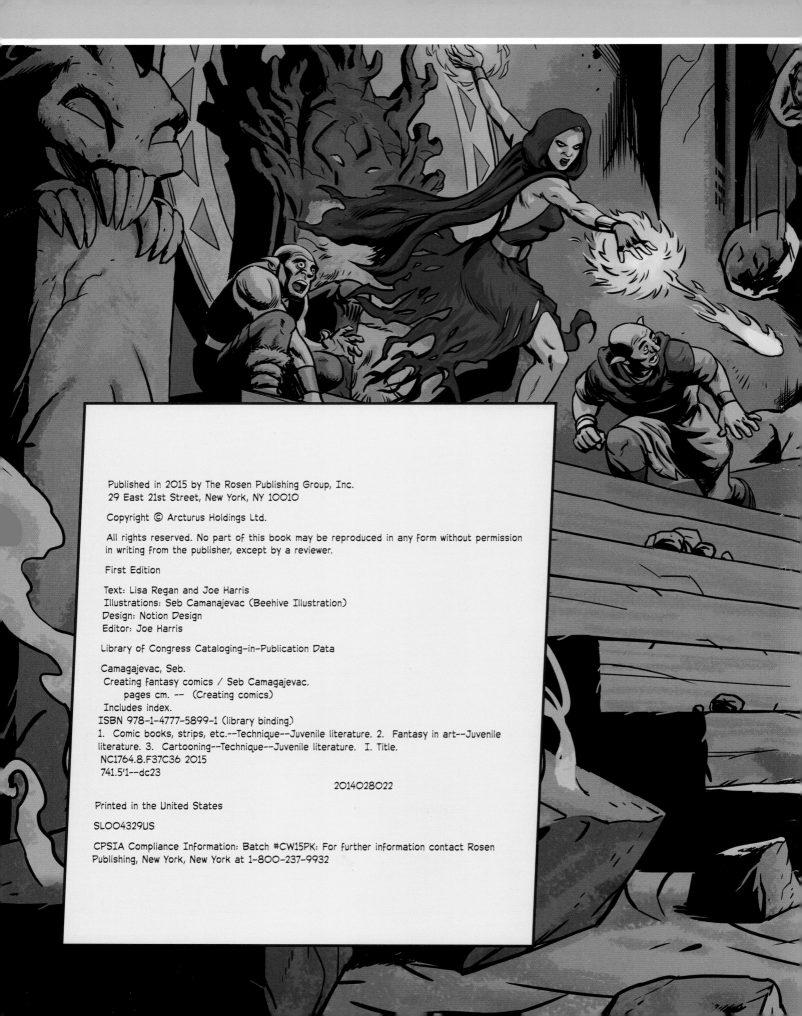

Published in 2015 by The Rosen Publishing Group, Inc.
29 East 21st Street, New York, NY 10010

First Edition

Text: Lisa Regan and Joe Harris
Illustrations: Seb Camanajevac (Beehive Illustration)
Design: Notion Design
Editor: Joe Harris

Library of Congress Cataloging-in-Publication Data

Camagajevac, Seb.
 Creating fantasy comics / Seb Camagajevac.
     pages cm. -- (Creating comics)
 Includes index.
 ISBN 978-1-4777-5899-1 (library binding)
1. Comic books, strips, etc.--Technique--Juvenile literature. 2. Fantasy in art--Juvenile literature. 3. Cartooning--Technique--Juvenile literature. I. Title.
NC1764.8.F37C36 2015
741.5'1--dc23
                                        2014028022

Printed in the United States

SLO04329US

CPSIA Compliance Information: Batch #CW15PK: For further information contact Rosen Publishing, New York, New York at 1-800-237-9932

CONTENTS

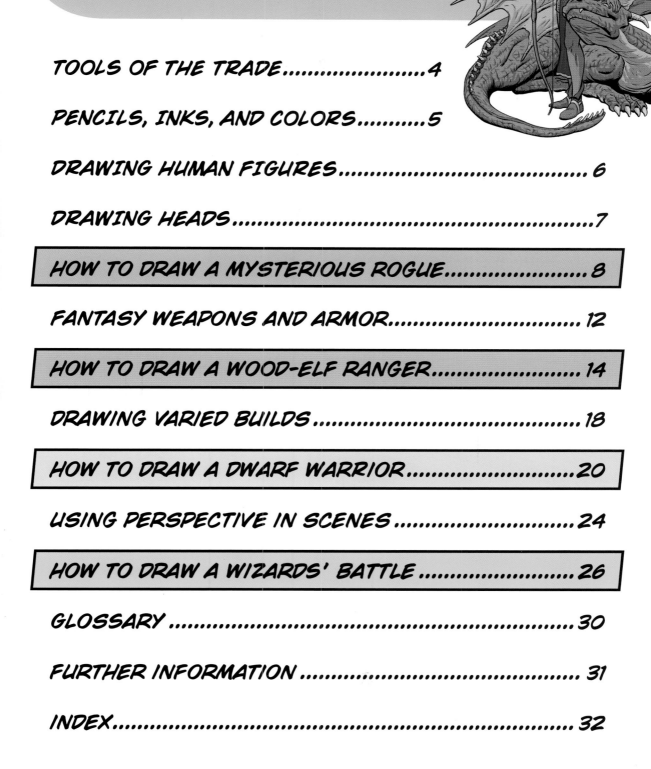

TOOLS OF THE TRADE

THE GREAT THING ABOUT DRAWING FANTASY COMICS IS THAT YOU DON'T NEED EXPENSIVE EQUIPMENT TO GET STARTED. JUST GRAB THE ITEMS BELOW, AND YOU'RE READY TO GO!

PENCILS

Soft (B, 2B) pencils are great for drawing loosely and are easy to erase. Fine point pencils are handy for adding detail.

ERASERS

A kneaded eraser molds to shape, so you can use it to remove pencil from tiny areas. Keep a clean, square-edged eraser to hand, too.

PENS

An artist's pens are his or her most precious tools! Gather a selection with different tips for varying the thickness of your line work.

FINE LINE AND BRUSH PENS

Fine line pens are excellent for small areas of detail. Brush pens are perfect for varying your line weight or shading large areas.

PENCILS, INKS, AND COLORS

THERE ARE FOUR STAGES IN THE DRAWING PROCESS. IF YOU FOLLOW THIS METHOD, IT WILL SAVE YOU FROM SPOTTING BASIC MISTAKES WHEN IT IS TOO LATE TO FIX THEM!

ROUGH SKETCHES

Start by making a rough sketch of your character. Work out their pose and proportions before adding any details.

TIGHT SKETCHES

When you are happy with the basic frame, you can tighten it up with firm pencil strokes, then add in some shading.

INKS

Ink over your best pencil lines. Vary the thickness of strokes and add dramatic shadows. Then erase your rough lines.

COLORS

You can leave your drawings in black and white, or add color. Your palette will consist largely of natural, earthy shades.

DRAWING HUMAN FIGURES

YOUR FANTASY CHARACTERS MAY COME FROM YOUR IMAGINATION, BUT THEIR BODY SHAPES WILL BE BASED ON REALITY. HERE ARE SOME RULES FOR PROPORTIONS THAT YOU CAN USE AS A GUIDE WHEN DRAWING.

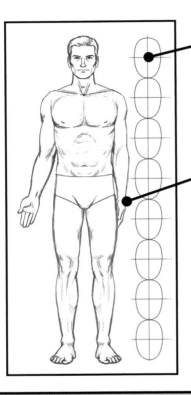

HEADS
Measure characters in "head heights." Typically, a person is eight times the height of their head, from top to toe.

ARMS
Make sure your character's arms are in proportion. Straightened, they should reach down to midthigh level.

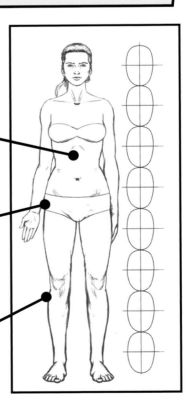

TORSOS
The distance from shoulder to waist should be about two-and-a-half "head heights."

SHOULDERS AND HIPS
Female characters' hips and shoulders are similar in width. Males taper from broad shoulders to a more narrow waist and hips.

LEGS
A well-balanced person's legs measure about four "head heights."

DRAWING HEADS

FACES IN FANTASY ART SHOULD BE FAIRLY REALISTIC. PRACTICE DRAWING PORTRAITS OF REAL PEOPLE WHENEVER YOU CAN. WHY NOT SKETCH YOUR FRIENDS OR FAMILY WHEN THEY ARE SITTING STILL?

MALE FACE

The eyes are set lower in the face than you might imagine—about halfway down the head. The face is roughly five eye-widths wide.

SIDE VIEW

Male heroes tend to have a square jaw. Add shading for the cheekbones, but avoid drawing the outline of the top lip for men.

FEMALE FACE

Women's noses and mouths are smaller than men's, and their eyebrows are thin and finely arched. Female top lips can be drawn in full.

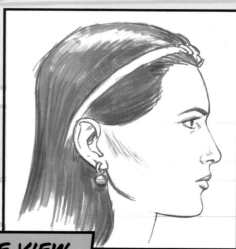

SIDE VIEW

Women have rounder jawlines than men. In both men and women, the ears should extend from the top of the eyes to the bottom of the nose.

A MYSTERIOUS ROGUE

"THIS KINGDOM CAN BE A DANGEROUS PLACE," SAYS THE SWORDSMAN, "AND IF YOU'RE SETTING OFF ON A QUEST, THEN YOU'LL NEED A GUIDE." YOUR FIRST CHALLENGE IS TO CAPTURE THE IMAGE OF THIS FRIENDLY STRANGER. HIS NAME IS REX, AND HE'S A DANGEROUS ROGUE!

1 Sketch a wireframe to show your character's confident stance. Make sure you get his body proportions right.

2 Loosely pencil in the shape of his limbs, using long, sweeping strokes. Add lines to show the curve of his chest. Draw a cross on his head to show which way it is facing.

3 Now your imagination can kick in. What is this character thinking? What is he wearing? Where is he going? How does he fit into your story? Our rogue is clothed for the outdoors, with a money pouch on his belt. Is he setting off on a quest?

4 Firm up your lines, and erase any light sketching you no longer need. Show the folds of the cloak and the creases in his leather boots. Spend some time on his face to get his expression right. You can sense the twinkle in his eye.

5 At the inking stage, use bold strokes for the outline and smaller, lighter strokes to show texture. Leave sections of his hair unshaded, where the light hits it. The sideways glance, fine lines by his nose, and the twitch in his mouth give this rogue a wry, knowing smile.

6 When you add color, keep in mind your character's personality. This man is mysterious, so he wears colors that avoid drawing attention. Look carefully at the shadows. Most of the shading is in darker tones of the main colors.

FANTASY WEAPONS AND ARMOR

YOUR FANTASY HEROES WILL NEED TO BE WELL-ARMED! YOU CAN TAKE INSPIRATION FROM DIFFERENT WEAPONS THROUGHOUT HISTORY. YOU HAD BETTER THINK ABOUT SOME PROTECTIVE GEAR, TOO ...

BECOME A MASTER SWORDMAKER

You can give your fantasy art a realistic edge by thinking about the details of your characters' equipment. Not all swords are made the same way! What kind of blades and hilts will your characters' swords have?

STRAIGHT SWORDS

A short sword (near left) is made for thrusting, and it may have a guard to protect the hand. A long sword (far left) is swung with both hands, so it needs a long handle.

CURVED SWORDS

Cutlasses (right) have a wide guard and a slightly curved blade for slashing.

MAKE YOUR ARCHERY HIT THE BULLSEYE

When someone is using a bow, their arms are raised high, with the hands in line with each other. The rear elbow is pulled back at a sharp angle, and the head is straight but able to "kiss the string" of the bow. Feet are shoulder-width apart for balance.

POLISH UP YOUR ARMOR

The armor worn by your characters speaks volumes about their wealth, status, and fighting ability. It can also say something about their history or backstory: Where have they come from? Is the character a veteran of many campaigns, or have they been thrown into battle against their will?

FULL METAL PLATES
The vulnerable parts of the body are protected with heavy, stiff metal.

MAIL OR CHAIN MAIL
This is made of thousands of tiny metal rings.

LEATHER ARMOR
This very primitive armor is made up of breast panels, cuffs, and a skirt.

READYING YOUR SHIELD

You can really have fun with decorating shields. What will the emblem say about your character or their family? Small shields are used to parry and fight back. Large shields provide the best protection.

BUCKLER
This is a small, round shield, gripped tightly in the fist to deflect the blow of a sword or mace.

A WOOD-ELF RANGER

THIS FEISTY RANGER MAY NOT BE HEAVILY ARMED, BUT SHE'S NO PUSHOVER. RAVEN SUMMERGLADE IS STRONG AND ATHLETIC, AND SHE'S A MEAN SHOT WITH HER LONGBOW. IT WOULD TAKE A FOOLISH FOE TO TACKLE HER WITH HER DRAGON AT HER SIDE.

1 Sketch the elf first, standing relaxed with her bow in hand. Then arrange the young dragon's body and wings around her.

2 Go over your framework, adding the lines of the elf's body and limbs. Flesh out the dragon's tail and head, adding clawed feet and wings held in a folded position.

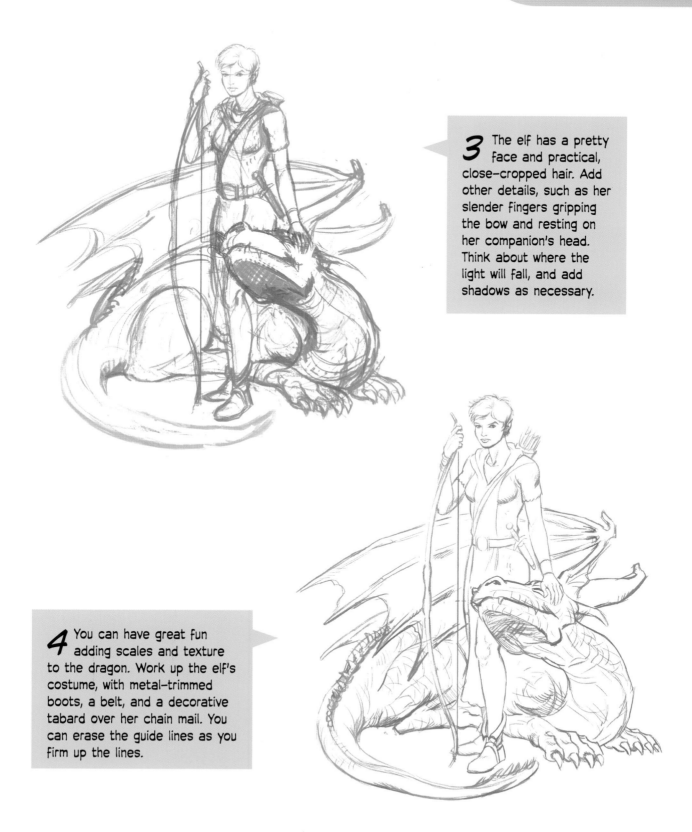

3 The elf has a pretty face and practical, close-cropped hair. Add other details, such as her slender fingers gripping the bow and resting on her companion's head. Think about where the light will fall, and add shadows as necessary.

4 You can have great fun adding scales and texture to the dragon. Work up the elf's costume, with metal-trimmed boots, a belt, and a decorative tabard over her chain mail. You can erase the guide lines as you firm up the lines.

5 Ink over your pencil sketch carefully. Use very fine lines for the elf's facial features. Each claw and spike of the dragon should be precise and neat. Don't rush! There are many small details involved, and you don't want to ruin your hard work.

6 You don't have to follow normal rules when it comes to coloring fantasy characters. This young ranger has dark skin but silver hair. Match the underside of her dragon's wing to the shades on its belly, with a deeper forest green on top.

IN ANOTHER WORLD ...

You can play around with alternative color schemes for your fantasy creations. Where they come from, there are no rules, after all.

DRAWING VARIED BUILDS

MANY OF YOUR CREATURES WILL HAVE A NONHUMAN FORM. YOU CAN PLAY AROUND WITH PROPORTIONS, CHANGING THE LENGTH OF LIMBS, SIZE OF THE HEAD, AND SO ON, FOR GREAT EFFECTS.

APELIKE CHARACTERS

This swamp troll has long, apelike limbs and a hunched posture. You can use this type of build for creatures such as orcs, goblins, and other primitive beings.

1 Start with a simple frame. The legs are bent and unusually long, and the body is stooped down low to the ground.

2 Flesh out the body, but not too much. The creature is thin and wiry—he looks hungry! Add claws and webbed feet and hands for a water-dwelling lifestyle.

SMALL CHARACTERS

Many fantasy stories feature characters with a short and stocky build, such as ancient dwarves that are as tough as nails. For the example here, we are using a halfling thief.

1 Here, the legs are only two heads high, and the body is just as compact. The feet look large in comparison.

2 Her body is bulky, but as a female, she still narrows at the waist. Her hair and clothes are shorter and wider than normal.

HUGE AND MUSCULAR CHARACTERS

Here is a foul-tempered, brutish mountain troll. You could use this type of heavyset build for big and tough but stupid and slow-moving creatures such as ogres, giants, and Minotaurs.

1 The troll has a barrel chest and rounded stomach. Notice how long his arms are and what a small head he has.

2 The lines sketched on his muscles add to the impression of strength and weight. Use plenty of definition on his limbs and body.

A DWARF WARRIOR

THIS WARRIOR WAS ONCE A MONK, BUT NOW HE'S LIVING THE LIFE OF A PROFESSIONAL MONSTER HUNTER. PATCH IS TINY BUT TOUGH AND WILL TAKE ON ANY OPPONENT, LARGE OR SMALL. THAT'S THE BENEFIT OF CARRYING A LONG—AND MAGICAL—SPEAR.

1 Use your frame to show that the character is ready and alert, with his weight on his front foot, poised for action.

2 Draw a cross on the head, so that you can position the dwarf's features correctly. Add outlines for his limbs, giving him strong—muscled upper arms and chunky calves and thighs.

3 Think about your character as you sketch in the important details. Our warrior has lost an eye at some point in his colorful history, so he wears an eye patch. He has a shaved head but an ornate beard, and the look of a battle–hardened warrior.

4 Now you can begin to remove some of your rough guide lines. Firm up the details and erase anything unnecessary. Use heavy shading to show the lines of his cloak and his sturdy boots. Finish his beard and face with fine lines.

5 For the inked version, use solid shading on the underside of his arms, chest, and chin and around the knees. Blacken his eye patch, and give his good eye a menacing glint. Decorate his buckles and spear to make them his own custom design.

6 The addition of color draws attention to the details, such as his pierced ear and the dagger tucked into a sheath on his belt. His clothes are shaded in muted colors, but there's no hiding his red beard and eyebrows.

USING PERSPECTIVE IN SCENES

THE USE OF PERSPECTIVE IS AN IMPORTANT SKILL TO MASTER. IT WILL GIVE A FEELING OF DEPTH TO YOUR SCENES, AND IT IS ESPECIALLY IMPORTANT FOR DRAWING BUILDINGS AND TOWNS.

VANISHING POINT

The straight lines in the scene all meet at a faraway "vanishing point."

PERSPECTIVE LINES

These straight lines show how the buildings should be positioned.

HORIZON

The vanishing point should be placed along an imaginary horizon line.

FORESHORTENING

Things that are closer are drawn larger than things far away. This is known as foreshortening, and it creates the illusion of depth. The buildings along this street become tiny in the distance.

24

Now imagine you are viewing a scene from below. The scene has one low vanishing point, across the drawbridge, and another high above the castle, which seems to stretch into the sky.

BIRD'S-EYE VIEW

This picture is drawn as if you are looking at it from high above. It uses two-point perspective, with two vanishing points in different places. Foreshortening makes the tower look smaller than the bird.

A WIZARDS' BATTLE

NOW YOU CAN PULL TOGETHER EVERYTHING YOU HAVE LEARNED ABOUT CHARACTERIZATION, PROPORTIONS, POSTURE, AND PERSPECTIVE IN ONE DRAMATIC SCENE. THE QUICK-WITTED YOUNG WIZARD, JARYTH, IS SHOWN HERE IN THE MIDST OF A BATTLE AGAINST THE EVIL QUEEN OF ASHES.

1 Decide on your vanishing point. Use the lines of the staircase to set up your perspective. Sketch the basic frames for Jaryth and the Queen, her minions, and the background.

2 Gradually build up the layers of detail in the foreground and background. Now concentrate on your characters. Jaryth is closer to the viewer, so he appears larger than the Queen of Ashes. Add in the details of clothing and the magical "special effects" for the fight.

3 When you're satisfied with the way the scene is shaping up, you can think more about textures and plan the way that lighting will cast shadows. Add detail to the fiery shield and the pieces falling from the roof.

4 The inked artwork is dramatic, with strong contrasts of light and dark (this is called "chiaroscuro"). There are no unnecessary lines or shading, but the viewer can spot details like the statues and hooded figures as they take a closer look.

GLOSSARY

CAMPAIGN (kam-PAYN)
A series of battles that are intended to achieve a specific goal.

CHIAROSCURO
(kee-yahr-oh-SKYOO-ro)
Using lots of contrast between light and dark.

EMBLEM (EM-bluhm)
A symbol that represents a country, family, or organization.

FEISTY (FY-stee)
Full of energy and courage.

GUARD (GARD)
(of a sword) The part of a sword that protects the hand.

PARRY (PAYR-ree)
To block an attack.

PERSPECTIVE (per-SPEK-tiv)
Showing three dimensions on a two-dimensional drawing, with smaller items in the distance.

POSTURE (PAHS-chur)
The position of a figure.

PROPORTION (pruh-POHR-shuhn)
The size of body parts in relation to each other.

VANISHING POINT
(VAN-ish-ing POYNT)
The place where perspective lines appear to meet.

WIREFRAME (WYR-fraym)
The basic outline sketch of a character, showing posture and proportion.

FURTHER INFORMATION

FURTHER READING

Davies, Paul Bryn. *How to Draw Dragons in Simple Steps.* Petaluma, CA: Search Press Ltd, 2008.

Frances, Tsai. *100 Ways to Create Fantasy Figures.* Blue Ash, OH: Impact, 2008.

Staple, Sandra. *Drawing Dragons: Learn How to Create Fantastic Fire-Breathing Dragons.* Berkeley, CA: Ulysses Press, 2008.

Various authors. *The Compendium of Fantasy Art Techniques.* Hauppauge, NY: Barron's Educational Series, 2014.

WEBSITES

Due to the changing nature of internet links, PowerKids Press has developed an online list of sites related to the subject of this book. This site is updated regularly. Please use this link to access the list:

www.powerkidslinks.com/cc/fantasy

INDEX